A to Zed of Aussie Slang 2015

Ian McKenzie

ISBN 13: 978-1503171060
ISBN 10: 150317106X

Contents

Preface

In November 2014, the G20 meeting of the world's leaders was held in Brisbane, Australia. Prior to that meeting, Australia's Prime Minister, Tony Abbott, announced that he had planned to "shirtfront" Vladimir Putin, Russia's President when they met face-to-face.

On the 17 July, 2014, Malaysia Airlines Flight 17 flying from Amsterdam to Kuala Lumpur, was shot down flying over Ukraine, killing all two hundred and ninety-eight on board. The majority of passengers were from Holland, but there were thirty-eight Australians on-board also.

Pro-Russian separatists have been accused of the downing of the aircraft. Continued fighting between them and the Ukrainians have made access to the crash site unsafe for investigators even four months after the crash.

It is claimed that Putin continues to support the pro-Russian separatists with weapons, and many blame him for the continued fighting and lack of access to the crash site.

"Shirtfront" had been a term known only to ardent followers of Australian Rules Football up until Abbott's announcement. It is now of course far better known. It means a rough bump to a player's front from a member of the opposing team.

At the time of Abbott's announcement, a spokesman from the Russian Embassy in Australia warned that Putin was a Judo exponent and Abbott should not get physical with him. Hyperbole is a hallmark of Australian slang. I am quite sure that Australia's Prime Minister had no intention of getting physical with Russia's President.

The "shirtfront" would amount to nothing more than discussions with Putin regarding issues related to the crash of MH17.

This "shirtfront" scenario though is an example of how language and its usage can change. William Shakespeare introduced several words into the English Language which are still in use today.

Colloquialisms, or slang, are a part of language. Language is changing, slang terms are changing. For example the terms, "tray", "zack", "bob" and "quid" were common slang terms used in Australia prior to the introduction of decimal currency on the 14 February 1966. The terms are used infrequently now. A tray was a threepence, a zack was sixpence, a bob was a shilling and a quid was a pound.

With technology making communication inexpensive and easy through social media sites and other media, there are global changes to our language and slang. The term "mate" is an Aussie slang term for a friend. I have heard the term used also in British television shows. "Fridge" a slang term for a refrigerator is used in both Australia and the USA.

In 2012 I published "Aussie Humour and Slang". The list of slang terms in that publication have been included here, but there are many new additions. In the 2012 publication, terms were listed in categories and the publication included many photographs. In this publication I have dispensed with all internal photographs and all the slang terms are listed alphabetically, so they should be easy to find. Some terms have multiple meanings and are therefore listed multiple times. To my knowledge this is the most comprehensive list of Aussie slang available.

Chapter 1 – The A's

A bit - Normally used at the end of a sentence as a gross understatement. "Bradman could play cricket a bit."

A bit of a – The person is not fully what follows "a bit of a" but has certain elements of it. "Fred is a bit of a fool." Fred is a little bit foolish

A bite short of a sandwich – Unintelligent. There are several Australian sayings similar to this in which something is not complete. The missing part refers to the missing part of a person's intelligence.

A quick snort – A quick drink of alcohol (normally beer)

A sandwich short of a picnic – Unintelligent

A stubbie short of a six pack – Unintelligent

Abo – A derogatory term for an Australian Aboriginal.

Abso-bloody-lutely – Most definitely – "bloody" is frequently used as an intensifier in Australian colloquialisms.

Ace! – Excellent! Great! Very good!

Aerial Ping-Pong – Australian Rules Football (AFL). The term is often used by Rugby Union and Rugby League fans and players referring to AFL in a derogatory way.

AFL – Acronym for "Australian Football League" – Australian Rules Football. More often called Aussie Rules Football.

After dark – Shark. This is an example of rhyming slang which was much more common in the early days of European settlement in Australia. It has many similarities with Cockney rhyming slang used in the UK.

Aggro – Someone who has become aggravated or sometimes aggressive. "Mary became a bit agro after constantly losing money on the pokies."

Akubra – A well-known brand of hat in Australia normally made of felt and commonly worn by people living in country areas.

Alkie – Alcoholic

All the go – Something which is currently fashionable. "After Twiggy wore a skirt above her knees at the Melbourne cup, mini-skirts became all the go."

Also ran – Unimportant or inconsequential.

Amber fluid – Beer

Amber nectar – Beer

Ambo – An ambulance driver or a paramedic arriving in an ambulance. Sometimes the term is used to refer to the vehicle itself.

Ankle biter – Young child

ANZAC – An acronym for the Australian and New Zealand Army Corps.

Anzac – The name was originally given to members of the Australian and New Zealand Army Corps who fought during World War 1. However, the term is often used to refer to any soldier from

Australia or New Zealand.

Anzac biscuit – Biscuits which were sent to soldiers during World War 1. They had good keeping qualities and were made from flour, coconut and golden syrup. Anzac biscuits are still very popular in Australia today and can be purchased from most supermarkets.

Argue the toss – To dispute a decision which has been made. Sometimes to just have a disagreement with.

Argy-bargy – Being argumentative.

Arse – Good luck. "Being made redundant and getting a great remuneration package when you were about to resign anyway, was a real bit of arse."

Arsey – Lucky. "You arsey bastard, winning that car in the art union".

Arvo – Afternoon

As busy as a cat burying shit – Very busy.

As dry as a dead dingo's donger – Extremely dry. A "dingo" is a dog which is native to Australia, and "donger" is a colloquial term for a penis.

As dry as a Nun's nasty – Extremely dry. Generally referring to property after a drought. Sometimes, "As dry as a Nun's cunt" is used as an alternative.

As fit as a Mallee bull – Someone who is very strong and healthy.

As Flash as a Rat with a Gold Tooth – Someone showing off or well dressed.

As full as a goog – Really drunk. A "goog" is a colloquial expression for an egg. Obviously there is little extra room inside an eggshell.

The term "full as a goog" can also refer to having had too much to eat.

As mean as Cat's piss – Someone who is very stingy or mean.

Aunty – The Australian Broadcasting Corporation, formerly called the Australian Broadcasting Commission. (ABC). The ABC is Australia's national broadcaster. Unlike commercial radio and TV stations it is advertisement free.

Aussie (pronounced Ozzie) – A true blue Australian.

Aussie battler – An everyday Australian trying to make ends meet.

Aussie salute – Brushing flies away from your face with your hand

Aussie, Aussie, Aussie, Oi, Oi, Oi – A cheering chant often heard by Australian barrackers at international sporting events.

Avago – Have a go. Usually followed by "ya mug".

Ave a go, ya mug – Words of encouragement, sometimes shouted at to a batsman at a cricket match. Sometimes used to encourage someone to act foolishly.

Average – Colloquially used referring to something which is not very good. "His performance on the football field was a bit average." He didn't play very well.

Avos – Avocados. Aussies often tend to abbreviate words. Many of our slang terms are contractions of the full name.

Axle grease – Money

Ay – Sometimes added at the end of a sentence, especially by people in rural areas. "It's a hot day to-day, ay."

Chapter 2 – The B' s

B & S – Bachelor and Spinster ball. Held in community halls or wool sheds in country areas, and usually associated with the drinking of large quantities of alcohol.

Back blocks – Usually referring to the outer suburbs in a city. The term can also refer to rural acreage close to city areas.

Back of Bourke – A very long way away. Bourke is a small Australian town in north-west New South Wales. It is about 800 kilometres from the State's capital Sydney and is often considered to be the gateway to outback Australia which lies to the north and west of Bourke.

Backchat – To talk back to someone in a cheeky or rude manner.

Backdoor bandit – A derogatory term for a homosexual male.

Backroom waltz – Interrogation at a police station
Bad egg – A person with a very dubious character. Often used to refer to a conman or a thief.

Bad trot – Having a string of bad luck. "First of all Joe was off work with his broken leg, then his wife Mary was diagnosed with breast cancer. The couple are having a bad trot."

Bag – To "bag" someone is to criticize them.

Bag of fruit – Suit (Rhyming Slang)

Bail (somebody) up – To corner someone physically

Bail out – Depart, usually very angrily

Baked dinner – A favourite Australia meal, normally baked lamb and vegetables

Bald as a bandicoot – A person with no hair at all

Ball and chain – Wife

Balls up – Really messed something up. A very poor state of affairs.

Banana bender – A Queenslander

Bang on – Dead right. "You were bang on with your answers to the test. You obtained 100%"

Bangaroo – Marathon sex

Banger – A saugage " It's time to put the bangers on the Barbie."

Bangs like a dunny door – A promiscuous female

Barbie or Barby –Barbecue (noun)

Barney – Argument. "The two children were having a barney over who should do the washing up".

Barra – Barramundi fish

Barrack – To support or cheer for your favourite team.

Bash – A wild loud party.

Bash somebody's ear – To talk at great length at someone.

Bastard – Although it can be used in a derogatory way, often

---

colloquially in Australia it is used as a term of endearment. For someone who has done well and gained some reward or success we might say, "you lucky bastard". Often used as part of a greeting for a friend we have not seen for some time. "How are you going you old bastard?"

Bathers – Swimming costume

Battleaxe – A derogatory term used for a woman. It may refer to an unattractive physical appearance or personality

Battler – Someone working hard on a low income and just making a living

Bean counter – A bookkeeper or an accountant.

Bean pole – A tall skinny person

Beat the living daylights out of – Administering a terrible thrashing

Beaut – Fantastic, great

Been around – Someone who is considered to be experienced. Often used with sexual connotations.

Beer gut – A man's large bulging stomach. The term is used whether or not the condition has been caused by beer drinking.

Berko – Someone who has gone beserk.

Bewdy – great – well done

Beyond the Black Stump –A long way away. The "black" refers to a stump of a tree which has been burnt by fire somewhere in outback Australia. Beyond that is a long way from anywhere.

Bible Basher – A Christian person who tries to get others to believe what s/he believes.

Bid Red – A large mature male red kangaroo.

Big ask – An unreasonable request.

Big Bikkies – Expensive

Big noter – Someone who brags

Big smoke – Term often used by country people when referring to the city.

Big-note oneself – Brag about oneself, boast a lot about oneself

Bikkie – Biscuit

Bikkies - Money

Billabong – A watering hole. Often a part of a river left after a drought.

Billy – A metal container hung over or placed on the camp fire to make a cup of tea.

Billy cart – A child's small play cart usually made from an old wooden fruit box using wheels from a discarded baby stroller.

Bingle – Motor vehicle accident.

Bite – To respond aggressively or argumentatively to something that has been said.

Bite your bum – I totally disagree with your request or proposition. Similar to "get lost", "go to hell" and " get stuffed".

Bities – Biting annoying insects.

Bitzer – A mongrel dog or any animal or person of mixed stock. Also "bitser" as an informal pronunciation of "bits of" as in "bits of this and bits of that".

Bizzo – Business

Blackfella – Aboriginal English term. As a noun it refers to an Indigenous Australian. As an adjective it refers to characteristics of Indigenous Australians. *Blackfella customs, blackfella talk.*

Bloke – A male

Blood's worth bottling – Phrase used for someone who has done a great job, or has been very helpful. "Thanks very much for your help. Your blood's worth bottling."

Bloody hell – An exclamation of surprise or displeasure. "Bloody hell, the power has gone out again."

Bloody –Normally used as an intensifier signifying approval. "It's bloody marvelous." Sometimes it is used as an intensifier signifying disapproval. "You are a bloody bastard."

Bloody oath –That's right. It is absolutely true. "Bloody oath I came first in the race."

Bloody well – Another intensifier. "You will bloody well do as you are told."

Blow in the bag – A test of the breath to determine the amount of alcohol in the bloodstream, usually made by police.

Blow that – Something that you could not be bothered doing. "I'm not going to study tonight. Blow that, I'm going out."

Blowie – A large blow fly

Bludge – To take it easy by not working.

Bludger – A lazy person who does not want to work.

Blue – To have a fight or disagreement. "Peter had a blue with his wife this morning."

Bluey – A person with red hair.

Bluey – A swag or blanket roll.

Bluey – A traffic ticket

Bluey – An Australian blue cattle dog. "Bluey" is also used in referring to stinging bluebottles found in the ocean and sometimes also to varieties of jellyfish.

Bob's your uncle – It's alright. Everything is OK. Often used as an acknowledgement to something that has been said.

Bodgie – Something that is inferior or worthless. The term was also used during the 60's to refer to teenage and young adult men who were characterized by having long hair and wearing leather jackets. The female equivalent of bodgies was widgies.

Bodgie up – To make something which has defects appear not to have any.

Bog in – An invitation to start eating the meal. "OK, now we are all here at the dinner table, let's all bog in."

Bogan – A person who takes no pride in their appearance and may spend their time drinking alcohol and achieving very little.

Bogged – A vehicle stuck in mud or sand.

Boil the Billy – To make a cup of tea. "Now we have eaten lunch, I'll go and boil the billy."

Bomb – An old car which looks to be in poor condition.

Bomb – Can refer to a large amount of money. "Those new solar panels you bought must have cost a bomb."

Bombed out – drunk or affected by drugs. Can also refer to being unsuccessful.

Bondi cigar – A piece of floating excrement.

Bonnet – The hood of a car.

Bonza – Excellent

Bonzer – Fantastic, great.

Boofhead – A silly person.

Boogie board – A small surf board.

Boomer – A big male kangaroo. Australian singer (now living in the UK) Rolf Harris, had a hit Christmas song many years ago called, "Six White Boomers".

Boomerang brand – Something that you have loaned to someone that you want returned. I like to use good quality pens and always have one or two in my pocket when I am teaching. On occasions I have been asked by my students if they could borrow my pen to sign the roll or some other document. Often when giving them the pen and explaining to the student that it is "boomerang brand" I am given a blank look. I then explain, "boomerangs come back..., so does that pen."

Boots and all – Totally committed to something. Giving something your full attention.

Booze bus – A police vehicle used for catching drunk drivers.

Boozer– A hotel, or a place to have an alcoholic drink.

Bored shitless – Very, very bored.

Boring as batshit – Extremely boring

Born in a tent – The phrase is used to criticize someone who leaves doors and/or windows open. "Were you born in a tent?"

Boss cockey – The person in charge. The boss.

Bottle shop – The part of a hotel or liquor supply store where you can purchase take home supplies of alcoholic beverages.

Bottler – Something that is excellent or very pleasing. "My new camera has completely automatic controls. It's a real bottler."

Bower bird – A collector. Sometime used to refer to people who collect worthless junk. Bower birds are species of Australia native birds found across mainland Australia. The male Satin Bower Bird collects anything blue that it can find and takes it back to the female bird on the nest. The blue items collected could be lolly wrappers, bits of blue plastic, paper or whatever.

Boys in blue – Police

Brass Razoo – Money, usually referring to lack of money. "He doesn't have a brass razoo." He doesn't have any money, or he is very poor.

Brekkie - Morning breakfast.

Brick – Someone who is reliable and unselfish. "Jane is a real brick for always helping her disabled neighbour."

Brickie – Bricklayer

Bring a plate – Attend a gathering but you are required to bring a plate of food. Generally all the food is shared at the gathering.

Brisbanites – People from Brisbane.

Brizzie – Brisbane, capital city of Queensland.

Brolley – An umbrella.

Bronzed Aussie – A healthy Australian who is generally also good looking with a good physique.

Brown-eyed mullet – Floating excrement (normally close to where you are swimming).

Brumby – A wild untamed horse.

Buckley's, Buckley's chance – No chance whatsoever.

Buck's night – Stag party, a male party the night before the wedding.

Budgie smugglers – Male bathing costume.

Bugger – Generally just used as an exclamation. It is not normally used with its literal meaning, to have anal sex, in mind.

Bugger me dead – A more emphatic exclamation than "bugger".

Built like a brick shit-house – A big strong muscular man.

Bull – That's nonsense. Used similarly to "bulldust" and "bullshit".

Bull bar – See "Roo bar"

Bullamakanka – An imaginary place in the outback.

Bulldust – A fine dust on outback roads in Australia. When wet it can form into a type of clay which builds up on the underside of the vehicle and make travelling very difficult.

Bulldust – To exaggerate or boast. To tell stories which are far-fetched or untrue. Can have a similar meaning to "bullshit". See also under "Places" for an alternate meaning of "bulldust".

Bullshit – A contrived story. Something said which is considered nonsense. It can be used as a noun. "What you have just told me is complete bullshit". It can also be used as a verb. "Don't bullshit me."

Bully for you – Often said sarcastically in response to someone boasting of some achievement.

Bum crack – The top of someone's bottom showing above their pants. Often used when referring to male workers on a building site.

Bum Steer – To give someone false or misleading information.

Bummer –A mishap or something annoying that has happened. "The battery is flat and the car won't start. What a bummer."

Bundy – A well-known and very distinctively flavoured Australian rum distilled in the Queensland city of Bundaberg. Most rum drinkers in Australia will ask for a "bundy and coke" not a "rum and coke". The term is also sometimes used to refer to the city of Bundaberg.

Bung – Not working well or broken. To cease to function. "The firm has gone bung, and the shares are now worthless." See alternate meanings of "bung" also under the headings "Behaviour" , "Anatomical" and "Aboriginal"

Bung – Something that is broken or not working. The word comes from the Yagara Aboriginal language of the Brisbane region. "The camera has gone bung." – The camera is not working.

Bung – The word is also used colloquially to mean to do something hurriedly. "Bung it over there on the bench." Or "Bung the ball over here to me."

Bung eye – An eye infection

Bung it on – Similar to "bung on".

Bung on – To behave in a temperamental manner, or in a way to get added attention. "She really bung on an act when she was told she did not get the part in the play".

Bunging it on – Similar to "bung on". "The extravert was really bunging it on just to get noticed."

Bunyip – An imaginary creature. In Aboriginal legends it was said to haunt swamps and billabongs (waterholes).

Burl – Attempt something. "Give it a burl."

Burnt offering – Food, usually at a bar-b-q which has been overcooked.

Bush – The hinterland, the Outback, anywhere that isn't in a city.

Bush baptist – A person who manifests little or no religious convictions.

Bush bash – Long competitive running or motorcar race through the bush.

Bush carpenter – A rough and ready handyman or a self-proclaimed carpenter.

Bush lawyer – Someone with no formal training in the law but with some knowledge of it.

Bush oyster –Nasal mucus.

Bush ranger –An intrepid Highwayman.

Bush telegraph – Gossip, rumours or any verbal informal communication network.

Bush telly – Campfire or the stars in the sky.

Bush tucker – Food from native Australian plants.

Bush walk – A trail or path in the bush.

Bushie – Someone who lives in the outback of Australia.

Bushman's hanky – Emitting nasal mucus by placing one index finger on the outside of the nose (thus blocking one nostril) and blowing really hard.

Bushranger – An outlaw. One of the most infamous bush rangers in Australia was Ned Kelly.

Bushwalker – A person who enjoys hiking through the bush.

Bushwhacker – A person who prefers to live in the bush.

Bushy – A person who spends a lot of their time in the bush.

Butcher's Hook – Look. Noun - to take a look. "Let's have a butcher's hook".

Butchers – The staff at a shop selling meat. Normally the meat has been cut/sliced/processed on the premises. The term also refers to the shop itself.

By crickey – An expression of surprise.

BYO – An acronym standing for "Bring Your Own". It can refer to unlicensed restaurants and also private parties bar-b-q's etc., where you are required to supply your own alcoholic drinks.

Chapter 3 – The C' s

Cab Sav – A contraction of Cabernet Sauvignon. A variety of wine. The term "Cab Sav" may refer to having a glass of the wine or purchasing a bottle. Many Australian colloquial terms are contractions or abbreviations of the correct word or words.

Cactus – Out or order, broken, does not work anymore.

Camp – Is a term used to refer to a homosexual person.

Camp - There are numerous meanings for the word "camp". However the way it is used in "Waltzing Matilda" refers to a temporary place to stop for the night. Drovers and others travelling in the bush would set up primitive cooking facilities "a camp fire" to "boil the billy" and sometimes some basic shelter. In Banjo Patterson's song, the swagman camped by a billabong.

Can of Worms – Starting something which is really distasteful or undesirable. "By mentioning the issues you just have there will very likely be repercussions, you have opened a real can of worms." Sometimes "bag of worms" is used instead of "can of worms".

Can talk under wet cement – Someone who never shuts up.

Cane toad – A person from Queensland. Cane toads were originally brought into the country to control the cane beetle in Queensland's cane fields. It was not such a good idea, as the cane toad has now moved over most of the Australian continent killing many native species as it does so.

Captain Cook – Look. Similar to "butcher's hook".

Cark it – To die, To cease functioning. Something that has stopped working.

Carked it – To die. To cease to function. "Because you forgot to replace the motor oil in the car, the engine has now carked it."

Carpetbagger steak – Beef stuffed with oysters

Cashed up – Having money to spend

Catch you later – See you later

Charge like a wounded buffalo (bull) – To charge excessively for goods or services.

Cheap as chips – Very inexpensive.

Cheap drunk – Someone who gets drunk very quickly with just a few drinks.

Chemist shop – Pharmacy

Chew the fat – To discuss an issue

Chewie – Chewing gum.

Chief cook and bottle washer – Someone who does the majority of jobs in a project. It can also refer to the supervisor of a project.

Chinwag – A chat or gossip.

Chip off the old block – Someone showing some of their parent's characteristics.

Chock a block – Completely full to the brim; stuffed; squeezed together

Chokkie – Bar of chocolate.

Chook – A chicken.

Chook raffle – A lottery, normally in a pub, in which the prize is a chicken.

Chrissie – Christmas time. "You won't get your presents until it is Chrissie."

Chuck – Similar to "Chunder" – vomit.

Chuck a sickie – To take the day off sick from one's employment when you're healthy. "Let's chuck a sickie tomorrow and go down to the coast."

Chuck a wobbly – Throwing a tantrum.

Chunder – To throw up, vomit.

Clanger – A serious mistake

Clapped – Worn out, of no further use. "Those tyres on the car are almost bald. They are clapped and need to be replaced."

Clayton's – Something which is fake or has been substituted. An imitation. It is from the commercial product Clayton's drink which was advertised as "the drink you have when you are not having a drink".

Cleanskin – Cattle which have not been dealt with as yet. (i.e. branded, castrated or ear marked etc.)

Cleanskin –Bottle of wine without a private label. Usually less expensive than privately labeled bottles, because the wine has been purchased in bulk by a wholesale company.

Click – Distance in kilometres referred to when travelling. "How many clicks before we arrive in Goondiwindi?"

Clout – Effectiveness. "The management committee does not really have much clout as all the decisions seem to be made by the CEO.

Clucky – Feeling maternal. "After seeing Jan's new born baby, Mary started to feel clucky."

Clued up – Knowledgeable.

Cluey – Knowledgeable. "With his experience in electronics, the technician was cluey enough to fix the problem with the computer."

Coathanger – In football, it's a dangerously high tackle with a straight arm to the opposition player's head or neck.

Coathanger – Name often given to the Sydney Harbour bridge.

Cobber – A close friend. The term "cobber" is mainly used by older generation Australians. It is not a term heard very frequently these days.

Cockie – A cockatoo. A species of parrot in Australia. Large flocks have been known to completely devastate a farmer's grain crop.

Cockie – A cockroach

Cockie – Outback farmer

Cockroach – A person from New South Wales

Cocky – A know it all

Cocky – A small farmer

Cocky – Shrewd or a smart show off.

Coldie – A cold beer. "After doing a hard day's work in the garden I really appreciate a coldie."

Colliwobbles – An AFL term to describe Collingwood's failure to win, having eight Grand Final losses and one draw.

Combo – Combination

Come a cropper – To fall. It can be a physical fall or it can refer to someone losing or having bad luck in business or in relationships.

Come a gutser - To have an accident or get something very wrong. "By not understanding the internal politics in the organization, Jack came a gutser and lost his job."

Come again – I beg your pardon, can you repeat that please.

Come good – Something which was not working now is. Can refer to someone being successful after a string of failures.

Come off the grass – Normally said to someone who is telling "tall stories" or not being totally truthful. "OK, now come off the grass and tell me what really happened."

Come the raw prawn – Lack of understanding of a situation. Often a pretended lack of understanding. "I think you understood what really occurred, so don't come the raw prawn with me, tell me actually happened."

Commy – A person belonging to or having sympathies with the Communist Party. Sometimes used in a derogatory sense for someone who is relatively less conservative.

Compo – Payment of compensation for someone who has been

injured at work or on his/her way to or home from work. Someone who is "on compo" is a person who is not working and in receipt of such payments. "Compo" is short for the term "workers' compensation".

Compo – Various mixtures of substances such as plaster normally in the building trades

Conch – A conscientious student who would prefer to study than to go out and enjoy themselves. The word can also be used in a similar manner for someone in the workforce.

Cook – A man's wife.

Coolibah tree - Eucalypts are endemic to Australia. The Coolibah is a member of the eucalypt family and is found throughout out-back Australia. Its botanical name is Eucalyptus Microtheca. It is the tree referred to in the Australian song, "Waltzing Matilda".

Cop shop – Police station

Corker – Something which is splendid or astonishing. "That was a delicious meal. You are a corker of a cook".

Corroboree – Originally used for an Aboriginal assembly of people associated with dancing for a sacred, festive or warlike occasion. Now it is used for any large or noisy gathering, or some noisy disturbance. Sometimes "Corroboree" is used to refer to the communal behaviour of some species of birds which flock to together and call loudly for extended periods.

Cot case – Someone who is debilitated, probably as a result of an accident.

Couldn't find a Grand Piano in a one roomed house – Someone who is hopeless.

Couldn't organise a root in a brothel – Someone who is hopeless.

Couldn't train a choko vine to grow up a dunny wall – Someone who is hopeless.

Counter lunch – An inexpensive lunch purchased from a hotel. Hotels in rural areas often advertise counter lunches for travellers passing through.

Cozzie – Swimming costume

Crack a fat – A male erection.

Crack onto – To pursue someone romantically.

Crack the whip – Get people to get a move on.

Cracking – Excellent. Also "get cracking" – get going.

Cranky – Short tempered or angry.

Crapper – Toilet

Crash hot – Something which is terrific.

Crawler – Someone who sucks up to their supervisor in an effort to impress them.

Creamed – Taken off a surf board by a large wave. In sport generally it can refer to an individual or a team which has lost by a large margin. The word is also used to refer to someone who has been beaten up badly in a fight.

Crikey – An exclamation of surprise.

Croc – Crocodile

Crock – An old incapacitated person.

Crook – Being and/or feeling unwell.

Crow eater – A person from South Australia.

Crumpet – Female genitalia

Cubby house – A small house in the garden or sometimes up in a tree which has been built for children to play in.

Cunning as a Dunny rat – A cunning, conniving and generally despicable individual.

Cunt – The external female genitalia. Also used colloquially to refer to a contemptible person.

Cunt-struck – Someone who is infatuated with a woman or women.

Cuppa – Usually a cup of tea, but can be any hot drink or beverage.

Cut lunch – A pre-prepared packaged lunch normally consisting of cut sandwiches.

Cut lunch commando – A member of the army reserve.

Chapter 4 – D, E and F

Dag – A person who behaves in manner which is not normally acceptable. "Dag" is also used to refer to someone with very poor dress sense. Sometimes used for people who are odd, amusing and behave in an eccentric manner. The word "dag" actually refers to the buildup off excreta in the wool around a sheep's rear quarters.

Daks – Men's trousers

Damper – Bush bread which was traditionally cooked in a camp oven over the hot coals of a camp fire. Damper is made simply from a mixture of flour and water without a raising agent.

Darwin stubbie – 2 litre bottle of beer.

Date – A social engagement with friends or with a single person with the intention of establishing or maintaining a romantic interest.

Date – The anus. Can also be used to refer to someone's buttocks.

Dated – To have anal sexual intercourse with. Also "dating".

Dead as a doornail – Something which is unquestionably lifeless.

Dead horse – Tomato sauce (Rhyming Slang)

Dead marine – An empty beer bottle.

Dead set – For sure – certain

Deadhead – A useless or stupid person.

Deadly – Excellent

Deadset – The truth

Deep north – Sometimes referring to someone from the far north in Queensland or can just refer to a Queenslander.

Deliver the goods – Do whatever is required

Demo – An abbreviation for demonstration

Dero – A vagrant or a tramp. "Dero" or "derro" is a shortened form of "derelict".

Dickhead – An idiot or fool. Sometimes used to refer to someone who has done something very foolish.

Didn't come down in the last shower – Someone who is pretty savvy.

Digger – A friend (a term of address used among men).

Digger – An Aussie or New Zealand soldier. Refers to the practice of digging trenches during World War 1. Also "digger' is used colloquially among men to refer to friends (cobbers or mates).

Dill – A fool. Similar to "dickhead".

Dilly – A woven bag made by Aboriginal Australians out of coarse grass or reeds. It was sometimes used in fishing and/or crab fishing. The word "dilly" is generally used today by Australians to refer to any small bag for carrying personal belongings.

Ding bat – An idiot

Dingo – A person who evades difficult situations or behaves in a cowardly or contemptible way.

Dingo – A wild dog which is found throughout mainland Australia and also in New Guinea. It is believed to have been in Australia for around 4000 years. Its call is more like a howl rather than a bark.

Dinkidi – Same as "dinkum" - The real thing

Dinks – Same as "dinkidi" and "dinkum"

Dinkum – The genuine thing

Dipstick – An idiot or a loser.

Dipstick – The penis

Divvy up – To share between various people.

Do your block – To verbally lash out at someone.

Do your dash – To throw a tantrum.

Do your lolly – To get angry

Dob someone in –To inform on someone.

Dobber – A tell-tale

Docket – A receipt for making a purchase.

Doco – A Documentary on television.

Dodgy – Something that is suspected to be unreliable or faulty.

Doer – A person who gets things done. A busy person.

Dog – A female who is unattractive

Dog's breakfast – A complete mess

Dog's eye – Meat pie

Dole – Unemployment benefits paid by the government.

Dole Bludger – Someone who is capable of work but receives dole payments because s/he is too lazy to look for work.

Domestic – An argument with a spouse

Don't give a rat's – Couldn't care less. Sometimes, "don't give a rat's arse" is an alternate expression.

Done like a dinner – Very easily defeated

Dong – A hit. "If that man keeps ranting and raving I am going to go up and dong him."

Donger –The penis

Donkey vote – A voting slipped not filled out to support any party or person. In Australia voting is compulsory. Donkey voters still need to register or risk being fined, but they can slip an uncompleted voting form in the ballot box as a donkey vote.

Donkey's years – A very long time

Doodle – The penis

Doovealacky – An un-described or un-named thing. Similar to "thingamajig".

Dorothy dixer – A question asked in parliament by a supporter of the person being asked the question. This allows a positive and propagandist reply to be made by the minister.

Down the gurgler – Wasted effort or wasted time or money

Down the plug hole – Similar to "down the gurgler"

Down the track – At some time in the future

Down Under – Australia.

Drag the chain – Someone who is slow possibly holding others up

Dreamtime – A term used by Aboriginal Australians. Part of their spirituality referring to times when the earth, plants and animals were created

Drink with the flies –To consume alcoholic beverages on your own.

Drongo – A stupid person

Drop your bundle – To give up

Drop your guts – To fart

Dropkick – A stupid person. Similar to "drongo" and "dipstick".

Dropsies – Referring to continually dropping things

Drum – Information, details of something or the facts. " Give me the drum about this function you have organised."

Dry as a drover's Dog – Extremely thirsty

Dry as a Pommy's towel – Extremely dry. A very racist remark implying that people from the UK don't shower often.

Dry up – Keep quiet

Ducco – A car's paintwork

Ducks on the pond – Warning to shearer's in the shearing shed that women were approaching and that they should temper their language

Dud – Something that does not work

Duds – Men's trousers

Dumper – A large wave that swimmers will not be able to ride and will dump them into the sand.

Dunlop overcoat – A condom. Dunlop is a brand that manufactures rubber products

Dunny – An outdoors lavatory – Often used to refer to any lavatory

Dunny budgie – A blowfly

Dunny man – Before the days of sewerage and when septic tanks were not common, the "dunny man" would usually call around on a weekly basis and replace the can of excrement etc., with a clean can full of wood shavings to use for the following week. The dunny man would normally empty the wood shavings and/or sawdust into a wooden box inside the dunny before placing the empty can into position.

Durry – A cigarette

Dyke – Water closet or toilet

Ear basher – Someone who talks too much, usually about uninteresting topics.

Earbash – verb - Constant talking on a topic. To harangue someone.

Earbasher – noun – See "earbash".

Earbashing – noun – See "earbash".

Easterner – *A Western Australian term for people from the Eastern States.*

Easy as pushing shit uphill with a toothpick – Something which is extremely difficult.

Easy wicket – Something that is easy to accomplish. Can also refer to someone who is in a comfortable position due to good pay and other conditions. "Since getting the promotion and the increase in pay, Bob is now on an easy wicket."

Egg beater – A helicopter

Ekka – An annual show in August in Brisbane. It is short for "The Brisbane Exhibition".

El Cheapo – Something which is cheap and nasty.

Emu parade – A group of people to pick up rubbish

Esky – Brand name of a portable icebox, but used to refer to all brands of these portable iceboxes.

Exy – Very expensive

Fag – A cigarette

Fair crack of the whip – Give someone a fair chance.
Fair dinkum – Similar to "dinkum". True, genuine. "If the bank is

being fair dinkum they will lower the interest rates."

Fair go – Give someone a fair chance. Similar to "fair crack of the whip".

Fair suck of the sav – Giving a fair chance. See also "fair crack of the whip" and "fair go".

Fanny – Female genitalia. In the USA it seems that the word "fanny" refers to a person's bottom, whereas in Australia it refers to female genitalia.

Feral – A person who is untamed or hippie like.

Fisho – A person selling fish and sea-foods often from a van parked on the side of the road.

Five finger discount – Shoplift

Fizzer – Something which did not work

Flake out – Rest after an exhausting task. To collapse or fall asleep.

Flat as a tack – A flat beer.

Flat as a tack – A flat tyre.

Flat chat – Very busy

Flat mate – A person sharing accommodation facility.

Flat out like a lizard drinking – Someone who is extremely busy.

Flick – To get rid of something or somebody.

Flick it on – To sell something for a quick profit shortly after you have bought it.

Floater – A turd floating in the ocean. In some parts of Australia it can also refer to a hot pie with mushy peas on the top. In Queensland it is generally referred to as "pie'n peas".

Flog – To steal something. *"The young boy tried to flog some chocolate bars whilst in the shop."* It can also mean to sell or attempt to sell something. *"The Real Estate agent was trying to flog off the low lying land he knew flooded."* "Flog" can also refer colloquially to the act of masturbation.

Flog a dead horse – To make useless efforts to raise issues which are no longer considered relevant or important.

Flog to death – To use repeatedly over and over again.

Flush – Having enough money.

Flutter – To gamble with a moderate amount of money. Often on the pokies or at the races.

Flyer – Female kangaroo

Footpath – Sidewalk

Footy – Football. In Victoria, "footy" generally refers specifically to Australian Rules football. In other states it can refer to any code. Soccer players will sometimes claim that their code is the only true "footy".

Foreman material – Someone who is dressed better than normal

Fossick – To search for something.

Franger – A condom.

Franger – A sausage. (A combination of frankfurt and banger)

Freak out – To have an extreme reaction to something.

French letter – Condom. The term is probably used more by older generation Australians. Many years ago when I was in charge of Physical Education/Recreation programs for a large community service organization, the gymnasts complained to me that the powdered magnesium carbonate chalk we had for them to rub on their hands before performing was not as good as the blocks. My research showed that the blocks had to be purchased from a French company which I had contacted. A junior assistant of mine at the time called Jenny, came out when all the staff and I were having morning tea one day and excitedly announced, "Ian, you have a French letter waiting for you on your desk." After the laughter died down, the embarrassed Jenny learned that a "French letter" is also a term for a condom.

Frog and Toad – Road "Well it's time to hit the frog and toad." It's time to go.

Fruit cake – Slightly mad. "Fred is as nutty as a fruit cake."

Fruit loop – A fool. An idiot.

Fuck off – Go away

Full – Totally drunk

Full as a boot – Totally drunk. Similar to "full".

Full as a goog – Drunk or full of food after eating too much.

Full as a tick – Similar to "full as a goog".

Full of it – Talking rubbish

Full on – Being enthusiastic or putting everything into a task.

Funny farm – A mental hospital

Furphy – Misinformation

Chapter 5 – G, H, I and J

G string – Knickers with a strap going up between the buttocks

G'Day – A common greeting. See also "G'Day mate". Sometimes "gidday" or "guday" are used as variations

G'day mate – A very commonly used Australian greeting.

Gabba – Short for "Woolloongabba" an inner city suburb in Brisbane where the "Gabba Cricket Ground" is located.

Galah – A fool. The name comes from a commonly found cockatoo coloured pale grey and pink found over most of Australia.

Galah – An endemic Australian cockatoo. Name derived from the Aboriginal term "Yuwaalaraay gilaa" for the bird.

Galoot – A foolish person

Game as Ned Kelly – Very brave or willing to be involved in risky behavior.

Game, set, match – A victory

Gander – To take a look.

Garage door is open – Advising someone that their fly is undone. Sometimes, "it pays to advertise" is said with the same intended meaning.

Garbage – An exclamation meaning, "what rubbish".

Garbage guts – A person who overeats. Generally referring to someone who eats almost anything

Garbo – A person who collects the garbage.

Gear – Clothes

Gee – Exclamation of surprise

Gee whiz – Similar to "gee"

Gees - Similar to "gee"

Get a Guernsey – Being selected for a position or task

Get a handle on – To understand something

Get on like a house on fire – To get on very well with someone

Get stuck into – To attack either verbally or physically

Get the nod – Approval to do something

Get your arse into gear – Get yourself organised

Ginormous – Very big

Gismo – Gadget

Give a gob-full – To speak your mind. To abuse someone.

Give it a break – Stop doing it.

Give it a burl – Have a go and try it.

Give it away – Cease doing something

Give it the flick – Get rid of it

Give me a bell - Telephone me

Go for your life – An invitation to enjoy something

Go to buggery – Get lost

Go walkabout – Wander off aimlessly or to lose concentration. The phrase comes from the Australian Aboriginal habit of nomadic wandering in the bush

Gobsmacked – Totally surprised

God Botherer – A religious person who tends to let other people know about his/her religion or religious beliefs.

Good as gold – Great!

Good oil – Really good information

Good one – An exclamation of approval. Sometimes it is used sarcastically.

Good onya – Good on you. A term of approval.

Good sport – Someone who behaves in an appropriate manner, especially someone who accepts defeat gracefully. The term is also used when referring to a willing female.

Good-o – Okay. Alright.

Goose – "you goose" means "you fool".

Got legs – Something that has the potential to become successful.

Grab – In AFL another term for a mark.

Bend the elbow – To have a drink, normally a beer.

Greatest thing since sliced bread – A great idea or invention

Grey nomads – Retirees touring Australia usually towing a caravan

Grizzle - To complain

Grog – Alcoholic drinks.

Groper – A person from Western Australia.

Grouse – Outstanding (rhymes with house)

Gunner – Someone who says that they are going to do things but never seem to get around to doing them

Gutful – More than enough.

Gutful of piss – Drunk

Gutless wonder – A coward

Gutser – To have a disappointing event or a failure.

Hammie – Short for the hamstring muscle. A footballer might "do a hammie" and not be able to play for a few matches

Hang on a tick – Wait for a short time

Happy as Larry – Very happy

Happy little vegemites – Contented children. Vegemite is a yeast extract spread made from by-products of the brewing industry. It has been a popular Australian spread for many years. When I was a young child before the days of television there was a radio jingle sung by a chorus of children advertising the product.

Hard yakker – Really hard work

Have a naughty – To have sex

Have a perv – To look at someone voyeuristically

Have a squiz – To take a quick look at

Have a sticky – To take a look

Have tickets on yourself – Someone who is egotistical

Haven't got two bob to rub together – Totally broke. A "bob" was the common colloquial name for a shilling in the days before decimal currency was introduced into Australia in February, 1966.

Heinz variety – A term also used to refer to mixed stock especially in dogs. Taken from the advertising for the commercial product Heinz soup emphasizing many varieties.

Hit the anchors – Put on the brakes

Hit the jackpot – To be very lucky

Hit the tin – Put money in to help with a collection for something.

Hollow legs – Eating and drinking a lot without putting on weight. Often used in reference to active teenagers. "Peter has a really good appetite, but he never puts on weight. He must have hollow legs."

Holy dooley – An exclamation of surprise.

Home and hosed – Someone about to win a race or come in first. Referring to a horse that has run a horse race, been taken home and hosed down whilst the other horses are still running

Hoon – A hooligan. Normally used in relation to reckless driving.

Hooroo – Goodbye.

Hop into – Get into it. Do the task.

Hostie – An air hostess – "Flight attendant" is the more politically correct term used currently.

Hot to trot – Eager to do something

Hottie – A modified car or other vehicle.

Hottie – A sexy woman. See also under the heading "Vehicles"

Howzat – An appeal made to an umpire in a cricket match by a bowler, asking if the batsman is out.

Humpy – A temporary dwelling made in the bush

I'll be a monkey's uncle – An exclamation of surprise

I'll be buggered – An exclamation of surprise.

Idiot box – Television

Iffy – Something dodgy

In good nick – In good shape. It can be used referring to objects which are not damaged in any way, or to people who are fit and healthy

In like Flynn – Usually used in relation to a successful relationship or sexual encounter, but can also be used in relation to being accepted in an organization or workplace.

In the bag – It's assured

In the nick – In jail

In the nuddy – Naked

In the poo – In trouble

In the shit – In trouble or when it is "In a shit" in a bad mood.

In your face – Someone who is very pushy of provocative

Iron out – fix a problem

Jack of all trades, master of none – A person who will have a go at almost anything but has no particular expertise.

Jackaroo – A male station hand on a large grazing property

Jack-in-the-box – Someone who is unable to sit still

Jillaroo – A female station hand on a large grazing property.

Joe Blake – Snake

Joe Blow – Just an average sort of bloke

Joey – A baby kangaroo

Journo – A journalist or newspaper reporter.

Jumbuck – Sheep

Jumper – Sweater

Chapter 6 –   K to Z

Kangaroos loose in the top paddock – Someone who isn't too bright. Unintelligent.

Kark it – To die (similar to "cark it")

Kero – Kerosene

Khyber pass – Arse

Kick in – Help out by contributing some money.

Kindie – Kindergarten

King hit – A punch which has been delivered without any warning.

Kiwi – A person from New Zealand

Kiwi Land – New Zealand

Knee high to a grasshopper – Someone who is very small

Knick – To steal

Knick off – Go away

Knock – To find fault with something.

Knock off – To finish work either for the day, or to take a short break.

Knock off time – The time work finishes

Knockabout – Someone who behaves in a casual way

Knocker – A person making derogatory remarks.

Knockers – Women's breasts. Normally referring to larger ones.

Knockover – A pushover

Knuckle sandwich – A punch in the mouth

Koori – An Aboriginal person. The word comes from the Awabakal Aboriginal language of Eastern New South Wales and neighbouring languages.

Lair - A show-off

Larrikin – A harmless prankster who likes to enjoy himself.

Layabout – Someone who is allergic to work. Similar to "bludger"

Left for dead – To be beaten or outclassed.

Leg opener – Alcoholic drinks offered to women with the intention of seducing them

Leg over – Sexual intercourse

Legless – So drunk that you can't walk or stand up steadily

Lezzo – Lesbian

Lifesaver – Lifeguard

Lights are on, but nobody's at home – Unintelligent

Like a hornet in a bottle – Someone who is furious.

Like a possum up a gum tree – Very happy. Can also refer to quick movements.

Like a rat up a drainpipe – Moving very quickly.

Like a shag on a rock – On its own. Very lonely.

Like a stunned mullet – Bewildered.

Like the clappers – Very fast

Lingo – Language

Lippy – Women's lipstick

Liquid gold – Beer

Liquid laugh – To throw up.

Loaded – Extremely rich. Having plenty of money.

Local rag – The local newspaper.

Lollies – Sweets or candy

London to a brick – Absolute certainty

Long neck – A 750 ml bottle of beer

Long Paddock – The vegetation strip between property fences and the road. The long paddock is used for grazing cattle during droughts.

Lurk – An underhand or illegal operation

Mackas – McDonalds

Mad as a cut snake – A deranged person or extremely angry person

Mad as a meataxe – Completely stupid.

Main drag – The main street through a town.

Make a blue – To make a mistake.

Make a crust – Work to make money

Make a quid – Earn some money

Mappa Tassie – A woman's pubic hair area.

Mate – Friend

Mates rates – Special cheaper prices for friends.

Matilda – A swagman's sleeping roll often containing food and a few other personal possessions

Melbournians - People from Melbourne.

Metho – Methylated spirits.

Mexican – A person south of the Queensland border.

Mick – A person who is a Roman Catholic

Milko – A person home delivering milk. There probably aren't many around anymore, but when I was young the Milko would call around each night.

Mob – Originally a group of sheep but commonly used to refer to a group of people

Mollydooker – A left hander

Mondayitis – Lack of desire to go to work on a Monday following the weekend

Monkey suit – A dinner suit

Moolah – Money

Moreton Bay Bug – An edible and delicious marine crustacean found in Moreton Bay in Queensland and in other northern Australian waters.

Mozzie – Mosquito

Muddie – A mud crab

Mulga – A type of tree growing in dry rough country. The term is used to refer to the country as well as the tree.

Murri – Another word used for an Aboriginal person

Mushroom – Someone who is kept in the dark and fed on bullshit

Muso – Musician

Nail biter – An exciting game

Nark – To annoy someone

Narked – Annoyed

Nasho – National Service

Nasty piece of work – An undesirable person

Nats – Members of the National Party. The National Party in Australia used to be called the Country Party. At the time of their name change there was a joke circulating that the Liberal Party are called the Libs, the Labor Party are called the Labs, but the Country Party wouldn't agree to their name being shortened so they changed it to National.

Natter – Idle chit-chat

Never saw the sun shine brighter – I am feeling great, never felt better.

Nick – To steal something, or to borrow something without first asking permission.

Nick off – Go away

Nicked – To be caught doing something you should not have been doing.

Nicky noo – Naked

Nifty – Stylish

Niggly – Irritable

Ninety to the dozen – Someone who talks quickly and continuously and does not know when to stop.

Nipper – A young lifesaver (lifeguard)

Nit – Lice

Nitty gritty – The hard core of the matter. "Let's talk about the nitty gritty."

Nitwit – A person who does not act intelligently.

No bull – I am not kidding or telling any lies.

No buts about it – It is not a matter to be disputed

No dramas – Generally used as an exclamation of acknowledgement like "OK".

No flies on you – You are on the ball.

No hopper – Someone who is hopeless

No problems – Everything is OK

No worries – Similar to "no dramas". Probably more commonly used.

No wucking furries – No fucking worries. This is a spoonerism like "Friar Tuck".

Nobble – Interfering with a race horse so that it will not run as well

No-hoper – A failure who is unlikely to be a success in life.

Nong – An idiot

Norks – Women's breasts

Nosh up – To have a good meal

Not a bad sort – A good looking woman

Not bad – Good

Not much chop – Not very good

Not my bowl of rice – Same as "not my cup of tea". I don't like it or want it.

Not my cup of tea – It's not for me, I don't like it. "I prefer to have someone else do all the bookwork. It is not my cup of tea."

Not the full quid – Unintelligent

Not within cooee – A long way away. It can refer to being a long way from achieving a goal. A "cooee" is vocalized long, loud, clear call rising rapidly in pitch used as a signal to attract attention in the bush.

Note – Legal tender, money

Nothing to write home about – Not very interesting

NSW – Acronym for New South Wales

Nudge bar – See "Roo bar"

Nuggety – A person of stocky build

Nulla-Nulla – An Aboriginal Club or Heavy Weapon

Nurse – In Australia to nurse can mean to hold. For example we may nurse a young child or a baby.

Nut out – To work something out. Generally involves collaboration between people.

Ocker – An unsophisticated Aussie

Off his (or her) face – Someone who is drunk

Off load – To get rid of something

Off the beaten track – Not the normal route to take

Offsider – An assistant

Old chook – A derogatory term for an older woman

Old fella – The penis

Old man – A person's father

Oldies – A person's parents

On the blink – Something is not working

On the turps – Someone who is drinking heavily.

One for Ron – One for later on

Op Shop – A store that sells second hand goods, usually run by a charitable institution.

OS – Referring to overseas. "Jim won't be back for three weeks as he has gone OS."

Outback – Inland away from the coast.

Outback –The interior of Australia

Oz – Australia

Pack it in – Give it up

Pack of galahs – A group of idiots.

Paralytic – Extremely drunk

Pash – A long enduring kiss generally associated with fondling.

Passed the use by date – Something that is no longer useful

Pav – Pavlova. An Australian desert made from meringue which is crusty on the outside and soft in the middle, filled with whipped cream and fruit. Named after the ballet dancer Anna Pavlovna

Penguin suit – Dinner suit

Perk – Fringe benefit

Perv – Voyeur

Pick someone's brains – To ask someone questions with the aim of getting intelligent answers

Pick the eyes out of – Choose the best parts of something

Pie eater – A person from South Australia

Piece of cake – A task which can be easily accomplished

Piece of piss – An easy task. Similar to a "piece of cake".

Pig's arse – I strongly disagree with you.

Piker – Someone who does not want to be involved in an activity.

Pill – Another term for a football.

Piss – Beer

Piss in the wind – To behave in an ineffectual manner.

Piss off – Go away

Piss up – A party with plenty of alcohol

Pissed as a newt –Very drunk

Pissed as a parrot – Very drunk

Pissing in someone's pocket – Flattering someone to gain some advantage.

PJ's – Pyjamas

Play possum – Play dead

Plonk – Cheap wine

Point percy at the porcelain – A male urinating at a urina
l
Pom – A person from England

Pommy – See "pom".

Pommy bastard – An Englishman

Pommy shower – Using deodorant instead of having a shower.

Pong – A rotten smell

Porky – A lie – Abbreviated from the rhyming slang "Porky Pie"

Porky Pie – Lie "He's telling porkies." He is lying.

Port – A suitcase

Pot – A 285 ml glass of beer in Queensland and Victoria.

Potty – A little crazy

Prang – A motor vehicle accident

Prezzy – A present

Pub crawl – Going from pub to pub

Puking – Vomiting

Pull your head in – Mind your own business. Don't get involved. –
Stop acting the way you are.

Pull your socks up – Smarten up

Put a damper on – To discourage something.

Quack – A doctor. The term is used to refer to doctors generally and
is also used to refer to unqualified doctors or those who are
considered not to practice ethically.

Rafferty's rules – Total chaos

Raincoat – A condom

Rainmaker – AFL term for a very high kick which does not cover
much ground.

Rat bag – A foolish person

Rat-shit – Does not work anymore

Reckon – "What do you reckon?" What do you think?

Rego – Vehicle registration.

Ridgy didge – Very true

Righto (or Rightio) – Alright

Ring in – A substitute.

Ripper – Beaut

Road train – A prime mover with several trailers attached.

Roo bar – A solid bar fitted to the front of a motor-vehicle to protect the vehicle if a kangaroo is hit.

Rort – A con

Sandgroper – See "groper" – Someone from Western Australia

Sangers – Sausages

Scratchy – An instant lotto ticket

Septic tank – Yank – Someone from the USA

Servo – A petrol station

She'll be right – It will be okay

She's Apples – It's OK.

Sheila – A woman

She'll be apples – It'll be all right (eg: she'll be apples mate!)

Shepherd – In football, to block the path of an opposing player.

Shirtfront – AFL term - Dangerous front-on bump. The term was only known by Aussie Rules Football fans until the Prime Minister of Australia announced that he planned to "shirtfront" Vladimir Putin on issues related to the shooting down of the Malaysian aircraft MH17, supposedly by Russian backed separatists earlier in 2014.

Shit-house – Toilet

Shonky – Inferior quality

Shoot through – To go somewhere else.

Shooting through – Leaving

Shotgun – The front passenger seat of a vehicle.

Shout – Buying a round of drinks

Shrapnel – Coins of little value.

Sickie – A day taken off work without the person being necessarily sick.

Silly as a two-bob watch – This was an expression my father often used when referring to people who were not very clever and/or did silly things. Decimal currency was introduced to Australia on the 14 February, 1966. Before that our currency was pounds, shillings and pence. The common Aussie term used for a shilling (12 pence) was a "bob". Obviously a watch which cost only two bob was not of much value and the term became associated with people who did silly things. It is probably now only used and perhaps understood by older generation Australians. *"Fred keeps putting down his glasses in different places and forgets where he has put them. He is as silly as a two bob watch."*

Slack – Someone who puts little effort into their work.

Smoko – Taking a morning tea break from work. Originally it was to have a smoke.

Snags – Sausages

Spit the dummy – To lose your cool as a result of getting upset over something.

Spunky – Someone who is attractive and sexy. Could be of either sex.

Squatter - In the early days of European settlement in Australia, people would settle anywhere on government land without government permission to run sheep and sometimes cattle. These people were known as squatters. Squatters were free settlers not convicts and the practice of squatting was generally accepted. In later years leases and/or licenses were obtained.

Stands out like dog's balls – Something that is very obvious.

Station – A large cattle or sheep property

Sticky beak – To look into someone else's business

Stone the crows – Exclamation of surprise.

Strewth – An exclamation of disbelief or surprise.

Strides – Similar to "daks", men's trousers

Stubbie – A small bottle of beer, normally 375 mls.

Such is life – These were the last words spoken by Bush Ranger Ned Kelly before he was hanged – The phrase is used to signify acceptance or all the not so good things that happen in life.

Swag - A swag is portable bedding rolled up with a few other minimal basic personal possessions and some food

Swagman - In the early days of European settlement in Australia, a swagman was a person who wandered around the country on foot carrying all his personal possessions in a swag on his shoulder. He would rely on gifts of food or money and do the occasional odd jobs for payment.

Sydneyites – People from Sydney

Ta – Thanks

Ta ta – Goodbye

Taswegins – People from Tasmania.

Tea – In Australia "tea" can refer to the evening meal or dinner in addition to the beverage. The meaning of the word is obtained from the context in which it is used.

Technicolour yawn – Vomit

Tee-up – To organise a meeting

The Lucky Country – Australia

The Never Never – The far outback in the centre of Australia

There are no flies on him (or her) – Said admiringly about someone who is quick and decisive.

Thingamajig – A thing whose name I don't know. Similar to "doovealacky".

Thoroughbred – Refers to pure breeding. In the Australian song "Waltzing Matilda", "thoroughbred" refers to the thoroughbred horse which the squatter was riding.

Tinnie – A can of beer

Tinnie – A small aluminium boat

To give someone curry – To give someone a hard time, to harass them or insult them.

To have a lend of -Taking advantage of someone's gullibility.

Too right – I agree. Most definitely.

Top drop – A good drink – wine or beer

Trooper – In the early days of colonial Australia, "troopers" were mounted police

Trooper – Someone who is genuine and a hard worker.

Trouble and Strife – Wife

True blue – Honest, genuine

Tucker – Food

Tucker box – A container with food. The term was often used in association with people traveling in the bush carrying minimal items.

Tuck-in – To enjoy a hearty meal. Often it can be an invitation of a host to start eating.

Turd – A despicable person

Turd – A piece of excrement.

Uni – University

Used beer department – Usually the urinal in a hotel.

Useless as an ashtray on a motorbike – Totally incompetent

Ute – Utility – Utilities are an Australian invention. It was designed for a woman to go to church on a Sunday and take the pigs to the market on Monday.

Wag – To truant

Waltz - Refers to walking or moving in a quick and/or nimble way. "He waltzed into the office and announced that he was resigning." The word "waltz" can also refer to taking something very easily. "He easily waltzed off with the blue ribbon for his prize bull at the agricultural show."

Waltzing Matilda – Walking around with a swag

What do you think this is, bush week? – You are asking too much, or what you are saying is unreasonable.

Wheelie – A noisy skidding turn in a car.

White maggot – AFL slang term for the umpire

Within cooee – Within calling distance, or close to. "I was within cooee of passing the test, but was unable to solve the final problem."

Wobbly – Unstable behaviour. "Throw a wobbly".

Wog – Someone of Italian descent

Wog – The flu

Woop Woop – Similar to Bullamakanka. An imaginary place a long way away in outback Australia.

Wouldn't work in an iron lung – Someone who is very lazy

XXXX – A brand of beer brewed in Queensland. (pronounced fourex)

Yobbo – An uncouth person

Your Bloods Worth Bottling – You are great or you have done a good job.

14310090R00041

Printed in Great Britain
by Amazon.co.uk, Ltd.,
Marston Gate.